Mesquites Teach Us To Bend

Mesquites Teach Us to Bend

Jim LaVilla-Havelin

LITERARY PRESS
LAMAR UNIVERSITY

Copyright 2025 @ Jim LaVilla-Havelin
All-Rights Reserved

ISBN: 978-1-962148-19-1
LOC: 9781962148191

Photos: Ramin Samandari

Lamar University Literary Press
Beaumont, TX

Acknowledgements

Several of the poems in this manuscript previously appeared in the following publications.

A Fire to Light Our Tongues, TCU Press 2022
An Amazing Eclectic Anthology, Western Mountain Press
Blue Hole
The Enigmatist
Mason, Texas Newspaper
No Season For Silence, Kallisto Gaia Press
Pure Slush / Life Span—Home
Texas, Being: A State of Poems, Trinity University Press, 2024
Texas Poetry Assignment
Texas Poetry Calendar, Kallisto Gaia Press
Voices de la Luna

Recent Poetry from Lamar University Literary Press

Lisa Adams, *Xuai*
Walter Bargen, *My Other Mother's Red Mercedes*
David Bowles, *Liminal*
Jerry Bradley, *Collapsing into Possibility*
Mark Busby, *Through Our Times*
Julie Chappell, *Mad Habits of a Life*
Stan Crawford, *Resisting Gravity*
Glover Davis, *My Cap of Darkness*
William Virgil Davis, *The Bones Poems*
Jeffrey DeLotto, *Voices Writ in Sand*
Chris Ellery, *Elder Tree*
Dede Fox, *On Wings of Silence*
Alan Gann, *That's Entertainment*
Larry Griffin, *Cedar Plums*
Michelle Hartman, *Irony and Irrelevance*
Katherine Hoerth, *Goddess Wears Cowboy Boots*
Michael Jennings, *Crossings: A Record of Travel*
Gretchen Johnson, *A Trip Through Downer, Minnesota*
Betsy Joseph, *Only So Many Autumns*
Ulf Kirchdorfer, *Chewing Green Leaves*
Jim McGarrah, *A Balancing Act*
J. Pittman McGehee, *Nod of Knowing*
Laurence Musgrove, *A Stranger's Heart*
Benjamin Myers, *The Family Book of Martyrs*
Janice Northerns, *Some Electric Hum*
Godspower Oboido, *Wandering Feet on Pebbled Shores*
Carol Coffee Reposa, *Sailing West*
Jan Seale, *Particulars*
Steven Schroeder, *the moon, not the finger, pointing*
Glen Sorestad, *Hazards of Eden*
Vincent Spina, *The Sumptuous Hills of Gulfport*
W.K. Stratton, *Betrayal Creek*
Wally Swist, *Invocation*
Ken Waldman, *Sports Page*
Loretta Diane Walker, *Ode to My Mother's Voice*
Dan Williams, *Past Purgatory, a Distant Paradise*
Jonas Zdanys, *The Angled Road*

For information on these and other Lamar University Literary Press books go to www.Lamar.edu/literarypress

This book is dedicated to

* Lucia who daily stitches the land we love
*the cats who see it all differently
and
* Henry David Thoreau who sharpens my eyes for the world

CONTENTS

13	WINTER
14	Yearsend
15	January Suite
16	Two Early Winter Haiku
17	Gather
18	Mesquites
19	the names
20	Still
21	Over-Thinking It
22	Wings
23	Silver
24	Composition
25	Winter White Here
26	The Same Grave
27	World Upside Down
28	caracara
29	Gnarled
31	INTERLUDE
32	Wreckage
33	SPRING
34	pre-spring
35	JoySpring
36	The Matter of a Mesquite Branch Too Big.
37	Not Birches, Not Frost
38	the miraculous is easy to miss
39	In Texas Spring
40	Juncture
41	One Bird
42	How We Became Better Birders
43	Grows There
44	Holy Cow
45	Their Variousness
46	wind haiku
47	bend not break
48	It Might as Well Be…
49	There Are Some Words Wind Forgot
50	Time Signatures

51	It Might As Well Be ...2
52	road runners' clack sound
53	Squawk
54	In Succulent Celebration
55	This is how it
57	INTERLUDE
58	Questioning the Muse
59	SUMMER
60	What Shade There Is
61	Some Insects
63	whines and rattles
64	A Window of Lace
65	I name the spider
67	Both
68	Betwixt and
69	Across
70	what music
71	Fore Tell
72	Prophecy
73	One Set
74	Peripheries
75	Links
76	Why the Long Face?
77	Of Horses
78	Cities of Nopal
79	this allure of days and days
80	Texas Genesis
81	INTERLUDE
82	Where Color Comes From
85	FALL
86	Geology
87	Transformation Haiku
88	Away
89	Into the Moon
90	October Ode
91	Listening

92	November Suite
93	Greys
94	Field Notes
95	see/seem
96	Locomotion
97	What I Might Otherwise Have Missed
98	The Unknowable and the Trunks of Trees
99	Dusk—Pastoral
100	Tree Census
101	Grieving
102	in animal darkness
103	Down
104	Fifteen Minutes
105	POSTLUDE
106	Recounting

WINTER

Yearsend

the year slinks out
sullen and cold
like a great blue heron
before flight
            contained,
solemn on an old field
staunch in his own
            beauty
            believer
in the grey of the world
even if
tomorrow's sky
            unfolds
from his wings
with an unutterable
                grace

January Suite

 I. Breezes

    the canvas between
    the horse stalls
     billows
       like a sail

    the horses, adrift

 II. Under the Weather

in cold January drizzle
the donkeys are lined up
along the fence

as if bowing to the weather
their heads droop
under the shelter of trees

they watch the traffic pass
my car kicks up silvery splashes
but they neither blink nor shiver

 III. Before

luminous January morning
silver light from a night of rain
   on blue-grey-green
     agave

a chord of cloud across the horizon

    lighter

all will warm
before this afternoon's
   burial

Two Early Winter Haiku: Open and Closed
for Joe and Linda

gardenia white

in this
winter
wind

blossom

Joe and Linda—

gift

*

fist of this flower
raised against the howling
wind
white—snow, laundry,
ghosts

Gather

low, dawning
sunlight on the studio steps
January morning
cool but with promise
    and the steps
    covered with
    a windstorm's
    leaf fall
    hovering in the light

gnarled large fungus
    pried from the bottom
    of one tree

    skirted by the leaves
    on the studio steps

    saved for observation
    drawing, a morning's
    musing

accepts the small warmth
    and the fellowship of leaves

Mesquites

how these trees twist
        and stay twisted
how they
        remember the wind
which turned them
                one way
and the drought
        bent them
the other

the earth they are tethered to
            dry and hard
the sky they nuzzle
        in their whorls and serifs

and the birds
that fly from them, nest in them
        come back to them
        believe in them
and all their
turning
                as I do

the names

how many years
has it been
since we called them
thunderheads
                      with all the
                      natural world
                      metaphoric
                      scary power
                      that's right there
                      in the name

                      the fear, the fire

replaced by scientific knowledge
or its terminology
names descriptive in their own way

                      leave us
                      bereft
                      of mythology

                      vitality

Still

                    how still
the rabbit sits
quiet looking maybe nibbling
but unmoving
for the longest time

nose perhaps wiggles
ear turn to catch
some sound
        but
for all that
sits stock still

it is the stillness
its concentration
and completeness
that makes the darting

after such measured
watchful quiet
quite so
startling

Over-Thinking It

rabbit's dash—
across the back, behind nopal, into the meadow, under
        the burn pile choked with weeds
under glistening, dripping, sun-splashed, dappled morning
light

too many adjectives
not enough
rabbit dash—

Wings

when the caracara passes overhead
the shadow of wings extends beyond imagination

        the first film to win an academy award
        for best picture, and filmed in San Antonio
        at Stinson Field

                dragonflies
                electric green wings
                and the thinness
                of lace

                        hummingbirds
                        gems of the air
                        their
                        hearts beating as fast
                        as their wings

                so many ball teams
                including the Rochester
                Red Wings of my
                youth

        Anselm Kiefer's lead book
        with lead wings which extend outward
        precariously, unknowing

at four a.m. the barn owl, after scouting the ground beneath the security light
looks right at me, spreads his breath-taking wings, and consumes the night

Silver

    Cold, January morning
                  and a fox glides
                                  across
    the backyard
    as we breakfast.

    sleek, grey,
                elegant tail - a curve, a curl
                    against
                gnarled trunks of the mesquite

                and the stones of the fire pit

    disappears
                into the over-grown meadow

                without
                          so much
                                        as a yip.

Composition

South Texas winter dawn light
etches everything even
brown grey flaxy grasses
that summer's blaze bleached
of anything approaching green

cactus silhouette, the nopal helter-
skelter rambunctious in the lightening
        sky

barbed wire curls insistent, purposeful
and the silky hair of the horses' manes
glitters – single lines susceptible to slightest
        breeze

the burn pile's a scribble beyond the cactus
and the blinds I peer through
set an understandable grid for all this chaos,
all this light

Winter White Here

is all air

        while the east coast
        is buried in snow

this white is all
an early fog
that hints at winter

and will be gone
by noon

burned off
warmer

The Same Grave

it always seems like the right place, quiet beneath a large tree
out back, to place a dead bird into a hole that will go unmarked
even when I forget that it's the same grave I've found
for each of the other birds that met window glass
and ended their lives stunned to feathered silence
at the side of the house after a sickening thud.

the shovel pulls away leaf rot and what might be
brittled bones of what is left
of all those birds, and I place him in, gently, sorry
about our windows, into the ground, the grave, layers of birds
in varying states of decomposition—it always seems
like the right place perfect, peaceful, even though
each time I forget it, and each time I dig
I find bones and feathers, and know that it is
the right place, because it is the same grave.

World Upside Down

sputtering in disbelief, silenced by the unimaginable
while nursed resentments boil unleashed under
      torch light

language throttled, twisted and felled so that
"populism" becomes a banner of hatred and
"states rights" means to right the ship of state
      with home rule

the meaning of meaning slinks off into
a darkness beyond understanding, gone
curiouser and curiouser—a flatland without
      warming

we shake our heads; our jaws drop
and out here in the country where I live,
their shadows large and moving across the land,
      hawks cry

carcacara

        falls
        from the sky
        is it

        drop or swoop,
        dive

        full intent
        fought wind
        and came down
        hard

        in his beak now
        prey
        was once
        alive

        scurried
        before
        swoop,
        beak and talons

Gnarled

the silent g is gusts of wind
how the mesquites turn themselves
twist limbs, contort
for rain or lack of rain
toward sun, or bent into that wind
they seem to dance
I hear the music of the wind
not silent - whistles, whooshes, works
its way through all our trees
why, even the stiff strong agave rattles
in the thrusts, but the mesquites
dance, turn, follow, and are frozen into
those gestures. I could read the stories
of seasons, years, in the path their limbs
describe. And you could see compressed
into the coiled trunk and limbs the power
to survive it all, by turning.

INTERLUDE

Wreckage

a poem that did not start out to be political
THIS is what the storm and breakdown
of February 2021 left us with:

a deep appreciation for showers and the flushing of toilets
depleted stock of candles, wax on the table,
collapsed cacti, sad to see: whole continents of nopal
those great green hands which raised their questions
to the sky tumbled onto themselves
a strewn deck of cards, a fifty-two pick-up
of spiny loss
and our majestic agaves
with spears turned yarrow white-yellow
and even the still green, with wrinkles
of stress on their once smooth spires

and phone calls and emails from friends
and relatives—concerned about how we were faring
fury at the politics of energy and how
they play out on lives
wreckage and anger, wreckage and clean-up,
wreckage and birdsong almost
saving us for spring
and after all of this,

to say nothing of what wreckage left
in the wake of four years:
lying, storming, pandemic, loss
all to be cleaned away with masks, vaccines,
and brooms and shovels
and axes and ballots and
memorials

SPRING

pre-spring

leaf skitter
across concrete blocks
in this brisk pre-spring wind
sounds like
a small critter moving
fast claws clicking
to find shelter
from the red-shouldered hawks
nested above, poised

JoySpring
in spite of it all

monday morning
an ooze of cows
           seeps
           over
     the lip of land
           beneath
     the ancient oak
on their meander
     to the far field
           beyond
     our meadow
festooned, choked even,
     with redgold flowers

what pandemic?

the Matter of a Mesquite Limb Too Big to Haul Off
Without Chopping First

how it must have—
                creaking
                snapping
      hit by wind or
                    maybe lightning

   leaning, bobbing in the storm

         a Macbeth or Lear scene
         in country, Texas

           aching, arching
           off the trunk

                  like all good mesquites do

   in the night and in the wind

              sighing free

              crushing wildflowers
              as it went
                        where it fell

   snapping, groaning, dry in the rain

                                —sounded

Not Birches, Not Frost

    sometimes
      the trunks
          of the mesquites

    without bark

    whitened by weather

        bleached out by
        sunlight
            battering

    look like bones

    and I walk, wander
        the rattle of

    this skeletal
        backyard

    one could do worse
        than be
            a singer
            of mesquites

the miraculous is easy to miss

that all the silverware
has its own place –
separated in plastic:
spoons from knives from forks.
a reassurance.

*

that something as slight
as the left-over tape
we couldn't remove
from the lid of the pot
we brought her soup in

can remind us of the dead

even if it cannot heal the loss

*

6 robins across the yard
of a friday morning
in march amid collapsed cacti
left by the storm and its
aftermath,

but who's counting?

In Texas Spring

dawn's light catches

mesquite
leafing out
  feather green, wisp green
  light lines of green
  width and weight of the pink
    lines of redbud,
  here and gone
  almost first of the flowers
and
thinly
in the air
    a thread scent of wildflowers
    sweetness until
    later in the balmy day
wafting
of barbecue
honeying the dusk

Juncture
Agave at the Window

       my window

       looks out
       on the great agave

       filling it
       square by square

I look into
the heart
of the agave

              where each spear
                    comes from

I know
in some part
of me

       this is where
       the world begins
              or ends

       this juncture, this burst,
                  this mandala

       this terminal
                  this branching

blue green
       fists open
              sharp fingers
                  emerge

One Bird

breeze brushes
long weeds
early flowers

March comes in
not a roar
in the window

and one bird
finds its way
down our chimney

caught, scratching,
echoing metallic
above the flue

listen to breeze
the wind chime
not the bird

scratching, dying

How We Became Better Birders

the western meadowlarks are back
practice, practice, practice—
                      the first year
we saw them, we were still in the thrall of
hawks and caracaras, delighted by bobwhites,
decorated with cardinals—we almost missed them.

looking more closely the following year, but with eyes
used to northern birds—
                      we thought some sort of
pale-ish odd robin
                and went on to the tiny joys of
bush tit and tufted titmouse.

one painted bunting and one bullock's oriole
blinded us to much else that year
                        and nesting red shouldered
hawks outside our kitchen window were the next season's stars

the western meadowlarks are back this year—
persistence, and that lovely lemony yellow, golder than that,
    breast, their trademark—
and persistence in our eyes
brought us around
                this is not to say the house finches, vireos,
and
inca doves didn't also capture our hearts—

but it was the recurrence—like seasons—
of these western meadowlarks
                      that instructed our eye
and finally, breaking our blindness to them—
                made us better.

Grows There

a bird or a wind
drops a seed or a pad
from the nopal
into a hole in one
dead mesquite

a niche above eye level
which the nopal
takes as home
settles in and
grows there

out of the wind
shielded, standing
safe, will stay
life force in a dry place
finds a way

grows there

Holy Cow

the brahma comes swaying
comes up the meadow
comes majestically up the meadow
toward the fence and toward me
in the half-light

the brahma's a lesson
in greys and in whites
blue-white
the white of carved stone
and grey to black, smudged

nods gently
all neck and wobble
in dusk and dry grasses
white of a light more
healing than bright

the brahma comes
swaying
all evidence of why
he might and must
be sacred

Their Variousness

earth, sky, rain, river, wind, water, sand, sometime
                                                                                                  they
accept the grammar
of the planet
                        but not accept
                        more
                        take in or are
                                      taken in—sheltered within it

they
                understand the rhythms of their world
                        something outside
                        under
                        standing
                                                          something

like
        mirror

                        and their time
                        and their places
                        and the marks they make
                        on the   earth

on their
bodies
                on bark

                capture
                        more like evoke   sometime

sand, water, wind, river, sky, earth

then   now

                        and not even
                        the space
                        of this

                        page

wind haiku

    a flock of feather
        clouds
    in a March blue sky
       which
    mesquite crowns comb
        clean

bend not break

another mesquite goes down
the rain-soaked earth won't
hold it, leaning, up

and that's ok, the roots still
in the ground, it may
where the trunk dipped
earthward, root again,

take hold. the problem
is in the crown, where
tangled with another
leaner, it is pulling at it,

pulling it down. leaning,
though not far away from
learning, needs that wisdom
which does not break, bends

It Might as Well Be...

some
spring music
    scratchy violin

sound of branch scraping
                             roof
in wind

tin roof   live oak
    spring wind
              jazz

There Are Some Words Wind Forgot

webs of ground spiders, silver with dew
        burn pile awaiting the end of the burn ban
where rabbits live under the splay of nopal
        footprint
                fence post
                        snake

even
        downed kite
                silent chime
                      mesquite limb

moss
        and
                wheelbarrow

Time Signatures

when I first moved here
I thought
that everything had
slowed down

it had not
I needed to slow
to learn, to know the rhythms

      the fan whirrs on electric, mechanical, constant, consistent
           while

there is enough variation in pace and pop
in this and that and them and those
to make Dave Brubeck
      smile

this is me walking the house around, stalking,
    striding, slowing
        that is the scatter of rabbits
          across the grass
them, the cows who lumber, rock across the far field
    while above them
        those hawks soar, sail, and sometimes
          swoop after critters

fast but sometimes
not
fast enough

It Might As Well Be... 2

    thrust into already hot
        if 80s in March is hot
    missing the wildflowers—driving too fast

    suddenly
    there's dust
    land parched
            cactus
            flourishing

    Texas Spring
    a moment before
    spring forward
            a blossom before
            hard pan and
            fire ants

    feathery neon green
            mesquite leaves

    rushing
    toward thick summer
    see
            a bluebonnet in my
            rear view mirror

road runners' clack sound from

        beak and gullet
        rattles across the yard

they dip their heads to bugs and lizards

woodpecker doesn't realize
our house is HardiePlank
not wood at all

        so when he rat-a-tats the beams
a sound like knocking
at no door
he gives up finally
makes his way
        vertical and pecking
        up the sides of trees

yes, the doves rustle up into the sky,
combined with their cooing
a mix of sounds before they

open their wings

Squawk

I'm so tired of these
ornery-thologists who somehow claim
I'm kin to dinosaurs.
        I'm not here to prove a theory.

Don't they know I'm the twenty-first
        century bird: speedy and sleek
        and outfitted with one sharp beak?

And while I'm flattered to have been made
into a cartoon character
        I have never in my life been heard to
        say "beep, beep!
my squawk is more like creaky door
        than the horn of some sports car

featherless, you hardly know us

so when the poet's wife tore up her ankle
        falling into a hole at Rio Grande Village
        bird-watching more than her step,
and saw three of us picking toward her
        our beaks hinging,
        it was not meant to threaten

more to gather, more to gab

In Succulent Celebration

we know the rabbits hide under the slowly sinking nopal
they manage to dart into the spaces between the pads
even in days before summer they find tunnels under flowers

cactus flowers used to greet us when we'd return from
each late spring's visit to Big Bend – quiet time before
hectic summer art camp. Now, I can watch them unfold

slowly, and just as slowly slip away leaving bulbous fruit
to ripen, plump and fuschia, sweet and full of summer.
I have sung the praises of nopal architecture times before

and watched them crowd out any words for elegant agave.

This is how it

       happens
mesquite dies
mostly
       uprooted
bark shed
and mesquite
       whitens
       goes
       to bone

Oh my graceful
       dancers
all that's left
       a bend
       a hand

Alicia Alonso
       still dancing
sight   almost   gone
had them
inscribe her moves
       her route
on the floor
       and she followed

sometimes
when one
       comes down
       a whoosh
       or slipping
       out of air
catches
my ear

INTERLUDE

Questioning the Muse

if, like the music of the gamelan, we are meant
to hear as we enter and as we leave
if the music is meant to continue outside us
before and after, and if you
cannot step into the same river twice, then
what is it we seek to capture
and what let go?

why is there a hole in our net?
how close can it get?
how long before it is gone?
seeped out like slow dawn, fog burn-off

if, as I know
I have at times mistaken
flaw for flow
and followed it out

let the words spill, spread, sink, or stain
in early spring's feathery green
the mesquites I sometimes claim as mine
are staking their own claim

SUMMER

What Shade There Is

the old horse
in August sun
and triple digits
will find
what shade there is

is in the recess
front of the house
so that
at least until
the sun moves and
the shade does
too

the old horse
faces the living room
window and
in the fever of
the weather
for a moment

you are Wilbur
and he, safe,
in what shade
there is,
is free to
speak
his mind.

Some Insects

1. the dragonfly I see
   on the screen
   bathroom window
   through raindrops
   steam and screening

   almost translucent
   could be a shadow

2. after I write a poem
   to try to stop killing
   the butterflies that
   smash into the windshield
   by the hundreds

   we arrive at Ward and Jeanie's
   and I find a dragonfly
   dead in the grille
   and irisdescent blue
   and beautiful

   is one death more important
   than another?
   can any poem save them?

3. the exterminator places
   canisters
   around the outside of the house
   terminals

   they think it's food
        he says
   they are drawn to it
   and they die

4. cicadas husks
   stick to screen and stairways
   hollow

not the part that clicks or sings
but maybe the part that
amplifies

5. the stick bug is
so fully articulated
and so camouflaged

I think
I get it.

Doesn't need a poem—
speaks for itself.

whines and rattles

       the weed wacker
       shreds the snakeskin
       without meaning to

       the snake
       sheds its skin
       naturally
                   a coiled mosaic

       the weed wacker
       takes its place, back
       in the shed
                   and

       the snake slips
       under the barn
                   into shadows

       much to the dismay
       of the family
       of rabbits
                   sheltered from the hawks

A Window of Lace

Out to mow under tree limbs, I'm careful
to avoid mesquite thorns, while
a spider web, all sticky threads,
enmeshes my face.

In further green thickness
I read another spider's construction
as a window of lace,
feat of engineering, a snaring place.

I name the spider

because I like the literary reference

and
I name the spider
because it's big enough
to warrant a name

and
I name the spider
because it does not just scuttle away
the first time
a lot of work on that wide world of web

and I name the spider
so that I can greet the spider,
acknowledge it

and I name
the spider
so someone else, hearing me address it,
does not just knock it down and step
on it

and
I
name the spider
to make the bridge between us
creatures different enough to never
make peace

Charlotte is the star of many photos
of our place
different people, different cameras
sent to friends
you wouldn't believe
        a spider so big it
                and them, they live harmoniously
                around it
                      step, past it

Charlotte, pointed out
named, no pet

regarded

Both

side by side
out our front window—
         spider lilies slender blossoms
         finger the daylight
                shiver in a slight breeze

inches away
    the great agave's
        blue-green spears
        over
            take our view
                filling the window
    with stretch
        and claw

things grow
        and sometimes in this harshness
                    things die

but here within one window
        delicateness and power

                both reaching

      in this place of so much
           helplessness

      it breaks me open to see
           this world
                    contains both

Betwixt and

                      trying to distinguish between coos and hoots

                                        doves and owls

                           between comfort and derision

                                  peace and wisdom

                                          every time I
                                    see the Whitewings
                                          take flight
                                          I hear them

take flight

                                       with a rustle

three times now I happened on
the Great Horned
and each time, in his own time
he has unfolded his massive wings
and flown off into the darkness
without a sound

                        on beyond observation
                        they are so freighted with
                        myths and mysteries
                        words and symbols and stories

no wonder
faced with the illusory human world
      they
              take
                      wing

cross

read across an enormous sky, panorama of my study window in Sunday silence
therings of cacti, horses and cattle meandering through to nibble at what drought's left.
ncing and fence posts - a few thick wooden poles, mostly metal and an open grid of it—
velinas can, we know, snort their way through, bending fence squares out of shape.
raggle mesquites and magnificent old live oaks at the far edge, some barn shed structures
w and far away, the occasional bale that stops the horses and cattle in their tracks to dine—
rn piles. a retama bisects my whole view, and the white tops of metal fence poles
nce mistook for birds, and waited in vain for them to take flight. By the time I have
talogued the world from my desk, everything except perhaps the grasses,
erything across my view, the light has changed, the day has moved on, and I have
ade some sense of how the X in the middle of Texas, spreads across the land.

rom "Four Texas Landscapes")

what music

a scissortail, still, on a swinging
strand of barbed wire, wings fill with early sun
and an idea of flight, potential
beholds me at the mailbox

the longhorn, somnolent, even benign,
faces the fence, quietly present—
and if with trunk and tusks,
could be Ganesh, and kindly

all on an early June morning
thickened air already pressing everything
"Giant Steps" on the radio
firmly in control of the air inside the car

Fore Tell

our front lawn
cenizo
      brought home from Alpine
      seasons ago
           and still thriving
goes a perfect purple
a dusty lavender
against thin green
           when rain is coming

desert sage
knows what will come
      more accurate than
      a finger in the wind
      or whether the cows
      are sitting or standing

less painful than
waiting to feel it
in my bones

Prophecy

the gatewheel will not hold
caked in rare mud after one rain
bumbled over too many stones
sprottling on the side of the wheel, not
a good way to roll

the gatewheel in a pebble dance
all askew, will fly apart and I'll be stuck
inside or outside, unable to move it
a calamity in scrub grass and mesquite

havoc and spot welding, replacement
from the farm supply store, or
standing in the full moon as the scrawny coyote
lopes by, knowing—this is what the Mayan calendar
                      meant

One Set

      a splash of red   sunset
      a slash of red   sunset
      a lash of red   sunset
      an ash of red   sunset

         ember   glowing
      remember   going

Peripheries

                    there
white horse galloping in dawn light
takes that gold in
and runs away with it
              under
the big tree
and off to where I cannot see

I can see now
what some people
find in horses
              this
       galloping gold

            *

last nightfall
across this
same scape

sky rampant with the fire
of sunset
        which ran across
        the whole west

from one edge to the other

licked at the horizon
            with
            fire

Links

    green lynx spider stretches a line across
        the twin towers of the cholla
            in front of our
              house

    every day I watch it cross back and forth
        a so-green head dipping
          working at it—crossing
            occupied

    while I gaze at arrow markings on
        this spider's back, and head
            so green it belies the
              season

    it is only when Mobi comes out
        to the house, that we
           learn the spider's
              name

    and while I imagined/remembered
        Phillippe Petit crossing between
           the twin towers on a wire
            before
            terror

    green lynx spider went about the work
        industrious in sunlight
        until finished and
            gone

    last night's storm—lashing wind and
        torrents, blew the spider's
            silky line away
              like
              that

    and I can only hope that the spider
        will
              come
                      back

Why the Long Face?

what do we know of animal joy or sadness?
      Sam's last dog morose over others gone
      and I watched school's beloved feral
          go all mopey and bereft
            over a partner's owl-met
              leaving
this was not the way this all began, more as a
      meditation on Mr. Possum, come
         each morning into the
           pool of security light
              to snuffle out
              some food
his long white whiskered face against his dark bulk
      my cats and I on the porch, watching
      and watching as he, heavy-haunched
          waddles away and into
            the dark
I wanted to ask him, not Old Possum of Eliot's cats,
      but denizen of the land of the house
          on the little bend—
why the long face?
      when the answer, not sadness or gloom at all
         but snuffle and discover
            my face is long
            enough to find
            my food.
one more question answered of the mysteries of
         the country night

Of Horses

never much
taken with equine beauty
having cast my lot with
cows, cattle egrets, coyotes,
even donkeys
                          it strikes me one
                          late August afternoon
                          the vision of the white horse
                          in the far meadow
                          framed by low branches
                          of the trees

the glorious rippling muscled grace
of the beast, and no metaphor
and grudgingly
I remember
                          those three horses
                          who leapt the downed fence
                          of their grazing lot
                          and ran like the wind
                          around our land

how those three horses
size and speed and simple dash
changed my idea forever
of the height of trees
the scrape of low limbs

a gallop's delight across
hardly open space

Cities of Nopal

For all of these Texas days and Texas nights
for sky we can believe in
and huge cactus grown from
one small pad
stuck in hard ground

grown into hiding places
for mice and snakes and birds
shelter from the heat of Texas days
apartment houses of serious needles
yellow flowers, purple fruit
from the predators of Texas nights

and almost human
almost hands
almost exuberant gestures outstretched and
knocking down the fence

silhouettes
a quiet city
against that believable and
believing sky

this allure of days and days

       enchants me
                      scatter of butterflies
       purple of morning glories
       and the twisting rankle of
                            our gnarled
                            mesquites

       see, I've made them ours again,
       ownership, a given
       but they
               grow and die and fall
               and are cut for wood
               for barbecues or
               planks for doors and mantles

       no one owns them
       they have as much their own minds
       and wills
               as butterflies and morning glories
               as all the weeds and groundcover
               and even though we put them there,

       the fences which
       over time and under birds
       take on a life of their own

               bent open by boars and neighbor dogs
               and over-grown with
               pencil cactus, morning glory, and
               plants I can't name

       peering over them
       rubbing their faces on the fence posts
       the cows
       drool

Texas Genesis

when the tree guy
proud of his kill
comes to show me
half a snake
wrapped around his hand
chain-sawed in the trunk
       of the dead tree
       they took down
I first have to stifle a gasp
of fear then sadness for a fellow
       creature, gone
and show him
some awe and congratulations
and respect
he tells me—
       it was living in there

and I know
even the left over squirming
that it is dead out here
curled over your fist
gripped tight to avoid
       one last bite

and I don't think for a minute
about Eve or Adam or apples
or knowledge or God or free will

just jobs, lawns, dead trees, hauling
hot afternoons, bringing him a Tecate,
killing with a chain-saw by mistake

the other half

Interlude

Where Color Comes From

drought
and then
some rainstorms

this desert flower
              that cactus fruit

we watched the first grow
before we knew it—
a pod
almost breathing itself balloon big

and then one morning broke open in a starburst
a slippery tentative green flecked with burgundy
slumped on the dirt

it could have been an anemone
an organ gasping
a token for a summer of deaths and sickness

wan, translucent, speckled, scored, a star—
the wine thickening toward the deep
unknowable center

              the fruit bumped off
              the top of the cactus
              where
                      it was learning the lessons of
                      precariousness

              fallen to the hard earth

              we picked it up
              brought it in the house
              before bugs or boars could get it
              sliced it open

              to reveal a pink-purple so deep
              it was a wound, a promise of sweetness
              a blaze across our eyes
              we did not eat

the brown grey ashen dry world of drought
lets color in
slowly
small miracles of a world without clouds
a sky the color of this new linen shirt
and sometimes
my eyes

Fall

Geology

the great rocks
seem to move
        ever so slightly
        at the edges
        of my
        western horizon

tinged in morning light
russet
        black
                and cream-marble-white

and then their calves
frisk out between
        them
and the rocks

morning light bathed boulders

turn into cows

Transformation Haiku

    paper clip could be
    a cricket, Basho's big star—
    a haiku staple

        snake skin as rubber
            band or garden hose, won't stretch
                imagination

    leaf as butterfly,
        bark—moth; what's a cactus pad
    if not a hand?

        but the computer
    mouse is not a mouse, as the
        lamp is not the sun

            when we see the world
                sometimes we see what we
                want to—
            not what we must

watch your step and hands
        don't pick up that curl of dust
            scorpions' disguise

if you go looking
        for creatures in clouds
watch out for your feet.

Away

the cottontails skitter-hop off
into the dark
under the barn

        neighbor dogs, giving up trying
        for rabbits
        squeeze back through
        the hole in the fence
        toward home

                and all four cows in the distance
                slip over the edge of the world
                and are gone

two horses appear
ready for us to ride
out of the picture

                the morning. watching.
                gets
                away from us

Into the Moon

cheddar round
big moon goes down
in the windows
of my study

our orange cat
tumbles down
the hallway

into the room
into the moon

October Ode

hay yellow field open in the sun
Van Gogh brush strokes surrounded
      by cactus, mesquite but no
      ocotillo

full moon—harvest moon
wide-eyed look into darkness
red orange glow goes down
      into that same
      field

one lone goose, honks, whistles
      left behind until
      one wind blows

cartoon mouth of cloud
      wide open in an "O"
      catches the goose
      and often a crow

      and blows them home

just so you know

Listening

    attentive
                    the rabbits
all across the back
sunlight
                  pinks their ears
    atwitch with
                  this minute

Durer attended to them
                      I do too
my eyes
            scan the sky

they go about their
                      business
ears always
            attuned

            for the hawks

November Suite

Off-rhythm

> the three-legged dog
> disappears into the glow—
> early fall morning

November Morning, Rabbit-Spotting

> It's the ears that are
> the tip-off, tell-tale sign that
> it's not a squirrel.

Election Day, Voter Suppression

> sometimes I forget
> who was running. But I know what
> they were running from

Veteran's Day for a Draft Resister

> I didn't go. So,
> I don't know what you went through.
>   and you don't know me.

Thanksgiving for Vegetarians

> Land which the pilgrims
> pried from the First People's hands—
>   they never held that way.

The dog, again

> I think I know the
>   rhythm of miss and stumble,
> and this, is not it.

Greys

In modest silver the winter days
troop out from late November
on the edges of one great lake.
The water will get pewter
      when the sky does.

Where I live now the sky is
almost always blue, the greys
are doves and rebel reenactors, but
the rattling coach of March in upstate New York,
punctuated by the stabbing whiteness
      of a snowstorm—

a black and white photograph
with greys along a scale—like notes,
a tune I can't shake.
                Recalls also those days
of greyed snow long into an interminable season
when darkness, a bleached shadow of
a man with a shovel, sound of scraping, all glittering
      gone, all that lasts.
      Salt grey.

I have grown old in a part of the world, this with
a glance across the sweet sane heads of my elders,
where what grows old
dries out and blows away, where
nothing greys.

Field Notes

    Now Caleb's placed the round of hay
        for them to feed at the far edge
        of the pasture beyond
        our meadow.

    I watch them gather. Eat.

        *

    who is left who remembers Paul Blair,
        Torii Hunter even, Pete Reiser
        hitting the wall

    outfielders of my life
    who caught
    everything

        *

    "At the field's end, in the corner missed
        by the mower,"
    can't ever get that close without
    tangling with the fence, so
    cactus grows up
    there.

        *

    my old friend, Lady Cow Vet, on her
    wildlife video feed, caught a glimpse
    of a bobcat, padding

    across her field.

        *

    field notes: speculative jottings to save
    for another time

see/seem

the white pony
        dashes across
                the far meadow

as we pull
        up the driveway

not purity, not innocence, not even
        glee

just
        the white
                pony

                              maybe not dashes
                              also not meadow, more
                                              field

and then
        there is what we
                make of it

white
        rambunctious
                leaping

yes, to greet us
        longing to be
                a metaphor

in tall grass

Locomotion

it is beepbeep the way the road runner skids
        across the yard
hummers thrum the feeder with disdain for one
        another
cottontails bounce across the back and into
        cactus patch
out of the sky the caracara is dopey looking,
        chicken-like in its taloned scratch
        mince
and I've told you how the opossum waddles

bobwhites the perfect bobbleheads as they hurry off
horses, cows, the difference in their center of gravity
        though foals and calves learn legs
        just about the same rambunctious ways

the woodpecker takes his insect-seeking time up
        the trunk and into the leaves, a careful
        threading his way

butterflies and ants the story's flutter, scatter
        solo, team, spiders and wasps, another story
        entirely

this leaves the acrobatic squirrel, hanging, stretching
'   all length and tail and try
        knocking seed
        out of the feeder
        mid-swing

What I Might Otherwise Have Missed

pinkened glow of sunshine
through rabbit ears

the froth of spiderwebs

varieties of grasses

death star mandala
      of the great agave
      after bloom, death,
      broken off
      carted away
all that's left

the industry of ants

snake on bark
      indistinguishable

the marionettish quality of
a stick insect

how the bend of fur-edged
      grasses in a soft breeze
      might be called
      lilt

mesquites' many greens
across seasons

The Unknowable and the Trunks of Trees

"just when I think I'm
free as a dove"
how and why bang against
a locked door

there are
I guess
some things
I cannot know

once
I made a list out of
a few of them, and put it
in a book

now I run my hands
over the bark
of the trees
in my west

mostly mesquite
all drought-starved
free from

all blame
any answers

I walk back
inside
reassured, even if
unsure

Dusk—Pastoral

walking back to the house
the grey sky of a grey day's dusk
lined, curved, with deep folds
slows my pace

too many days of too little sun
and we stop looking at the
nuances of grey, but tonight
walking back

to the house in a quiet
I could spoon into a dish
no cows, no horses, no distant
train or highway

this folded sky consoles me
a flannel sheet for a sleeping world
and yes, a dish of quiet
before slipping into bed

Tree Census

I met a man
Canadian
one April in
Big Bend.

He had
taken part
in his
nation's
tree census.

This seemed
a rational
idea, approach,
sane and
Canadian.

Today I look
out all my
windows
at all
my trees—

I know they
are not
my trees.
I have
established
that .

And in
golden
late fall
light
bending

they
wait
to be counted.

Grieving

I have read maps on stones for quite some time now,
learned their symbols and their ways.
Just what they say.
And while I know the world is filled with such unearthly
      sadness,
as makes just staying alive a hard task,
I also know the thrum of hummingbirds and the intricacies
      of Garcia Marquez' vision,
the turning of his words.
Heart-sick with loss the mesquite grows, bent in the wind.
And merciless, howling, it scratches
at the hard faces of stones,
and it makes
something I take
for a map.

in animal darkness

on beyond opossum
and possible rustlings

I thought I heard
an owl, feathers and hoot
and maybe even

the sound of cactus flowers
closing up shop for the night
withdrawing from

night's here and there and
hiding – what doesn't sleep
hunts here

Down

    the dead dancing mesquite
        has given up the ghost

    I used to love the gentle way
        it bent toward
            earth

    perhaps it knew

    the bend I see
        still

    an arc
        in the air
            of the tree
    that isn't
        there

Fifteen Minutes

        light spills silent into the trees
        morning gold touches the great oak
        on Caleb's land
        its glittering brush wakes the birds

        by the time the cows and horses
        make their way beneath embracing limbs
        the tree, meadow, cactus, our rooftop
        and all are bathed in light

        how morning happens,
        watch closely

Postlude

Recounting

Ten bobwhites in a troop beneath the tree.
One black and iridescent blue butterfly over the fire pit.
Squirrels, I lose count.
Is it one or two hawks the screech call flap and shadow.
Dove, whitewing, just one, bullet hole in its neck, and otherwise
       perfect, like sleep.

Four new bookshelves and still not enough space.

Fourth year now with them behind the razor wire.
New poems across a week gone thick with humidity, and
       I lose count. Though they are not squirrels.
Snub-nosed butterflies litter the air, if I wanted to count them
       I'd start with the splashes of dead on my windshield
       and multiply by one hundred.

But I wonder,

Do the dead count?

www.ingramcontent.com/pod-product-compliance
Lightning Source LLC
Chambersburg PA
CBHW060839190426
43197CB00040B/2696